BUILDING AN ONLINE DOG BOUTIQUE

Your Blueprint for Profits

GREG PREITE

ISBN: 1456385631
ISBN-13: 9781456385637

To my beautiful wife, Kimberly, without whom I
would not be in this industry and would not
be in a position to help others realize their dreams.

TABLE OF CONTENTS

INTRODUCTION

Just about everyone loves dogs, am I right? After all, who can resist the "smile" of a wrinkled-faced Pug or happy go lucky demeanor of a playful Maltese? Our love for our furry friends has caused us all to do some crazy things along the way- Elvis costumes on Halloween, a Christmas stocking with "Fido's" name on the fireplace (probably filled with more toys than anyone else's), Vet bills that we pay even when we can not afford them, and even specialty diets. Yes, the dog is the only one in the family that actually gets a specialty diet! Go figure. And here's the one that I really love… somehow, you planned on only one or maybe two canines in the household and all of the sudden you are finding yourself outnumbered. Your spouse looks at you as if to say "How did this happen?" but they know better not to say anything because some battles just must be conceded.

So now your crazy canine compulsion has culminated in a quest for cash. In other words, you are so in love with your doggie that you decided that the best thing for you to do was start an online dog boutique. After all, the only thing that stinks more than a day-old poop bag is today's job market! Everyone will tell you that to really succeed in business you have to find your passion and develop it. Since an online business sounds easy enough, why not combine your enthusiasm for pups with the power of the internet and start creating your fortune from home? Is that how this all got started? If so, you are not alone. Welcome to the club!

Before I go any further, I feel that it is necessary to give you a little background on myself. If you are going to proceed to the next page, you might as well know something about the guy writing it.

I can't really take credit for my existence in the online dog boutique world. That honor is bestowed upon my wife, Kimberly. She's a high school English teacher who just happens to be one of those insanely obsessive dog people. You know the type. If we are driving and come across a dog happily playing outside without its human, she is compelled to make me stop so that we can make sure that the dog is safe, has plenty of food and water, and can navigate itself back home. I'm relatively positive that a child playing alone wouldn't gather near as much attention. (Funny, I think I just heard a few of you laugh as you can recall doing the same thing at least once or twice.) Anyway, Kim's love for dogs is what caused me to take a hard look into this industry years ago when we stumbled upon Jack, a wonderful gentleman who was looking to retire and sell his wholesale dog clothing business. In the ten years prior to meeting Jack, I had built a successful career in the mortgage industry and had worked for large financial institutions. I really thought I had found my calling back then, but that was before the credit collapse and mortgage meltdown hit the entire country. The bank I worked for at the time literally was swallowed up in a sea of foreclosures and loss, and I was forced to look for something new. Enter Jack!

Now, my years in the mortgage industry taught me how to market myself, how to develop and cultivate business relationships, how to speak in front of hundreds of people, and how to close a sale. I figured that if I could sell a million dollar mortgage, how tough could it be to sell dog clothes, collars, and leashes? I had a professor my senior year in college who used to say "Sometimes you can be perfectly logical *and dead wrong!*" There is another saying, which I am sure you have heard, that simply points out that sometimes *"You don't know what you don't know."* I was right about a few things, namely that my sales experience would indeed help me to develop some critical business relationships in the dog industry, but the thing that I really "didn't know that I didn't know" was the intricacy of building a business **online**. Being able to capture the attention of a web surfer that I have never met (and probably never will) and actually get that person to pull out their credit card and spend money at my website was a concept that sounded so basic and simple to me, yet turned out to be incredibly complex. Luckily for me, rather than finding this complexity to be demoralizing and overwhelming, I found it to be fascinating. If you want your online boutique to really flourish and thrive, then you must have this same fascination and fervor.

So there I was, proud owner of an online store and pretty much clueless when it came to websites and the internet. Actually, defining my level of incompetence as *pretty much* clueless is giving myself far more credit than I deserved at that time. In reality, I was *completely* clueless. I remember one day during the summer of 2008 when someone told me I should start "blogging." Oh good grief, not only did this sound far too involved and difficult, but the only thing I knew about blogging was how to spell it, and that was a stretch! That idea went in one ear and right out the other.

Given the fact that my company, Doggie Designer, sells wholesale and also dropships for hundreds of websites worldwide, I had this huge database of account holders. Being the *marketing genius* (LOL) that I thought I was back then, I decided that it would be smart to contact all of my account holders, see how they were doing, and offer any assistance that I could. Therefore, during the later part of 2009 I set out to do just that. I started making phone calls, sending emails, and attempting to contact this list of nearly 2000 people who had all opened an online dog boutique within the past year and registered for an account with Doggie Designer. The result of this campaign was so shocking that it stopped me dead in my tracks. Roughly 80% were already out of business before they could make it to their one year anniversary! These were people who had spent thousands of dollars from their savings and retirement accounts to get started. They invested hours and hours of work into their websites. Some were even planning on this internet venture to generate supplemental income because they had been laid off or retired. A reality check for me? You bet it was! Here's what I realized in that instant...

Having an online dog boutique only guarantees that you will spend money, not make money!

People like to tell you we are in a "recession-proof" industry. **They are wrong.** People assume that if you have a website with a good product and a good price you will get tons of sales. **They are wrong.** And some people will think that all you need to succeed is a fancy site combined with a passion for dogs. **They are wrong too.**

Here's the truth...

Having a website is meaningless. Anyone can do it and, in fact, millions of people have. The key, and believe me this is 99% of the game, is being able to market your website effectively so that people can find you. If you can't do that, it's like having a lemonade stand in your backyard- no matter how good the lemonade is, the only ones that will buy it are a few friends and family members. When they aren't thirsty any more, you are out of business. The number one reason my ex-account holders would give me for shutting down was that they were not getting visitors to their site and they were not getting orders.

And so, my friends, this leads me to the purpose of writing this book. I have spent the last year and a half of my life learning how to effectively market online. I have talked with dozens and dozens of frustrated boutique owners and discovered their challenges. I have developed my skills in ways that I never thought I would. Yes, I can now even spell B-L-O-G. I have watched way too many people waste way too much money only to disappear way too quickly- sometimes before they even get started. This book offers you the truth. It's not some fancy piece of propaganda designed to convince you of how easy it is to start an online business. It's not a "fluff" piece intended to sugar coat reality or tell you that I can "Get you to page one of Google." It is a reference manual that will take you from ground zero with your online dog boutique and give you a strategic, proven plan for success. My goal is that you keep next to your computer and learn something new every time you pick it up. Yes, some of the concepts may be more difficult than others, but unlike most reference books, I promise to keep you entertained, keep it interesting, and keep is simple.

Hey, I've "been there, done that" and now it is my turn to share my knowledge, my experiences, my successes, and my failures with you, in hopes that your path to your dreams and goals might be just a little bit shorter.

To your success,

Greg

GETTING STARTED

Who Should Read This Book

There are literally thousands of people (if not more) holding on to the dream of building a giant business online, running it from home, and attaining freedom from the everyday grind of a job. If you find yourself in this boat, realize that the strong dream is a must, but equally important is a blueprint. Any viable project or venture starts with a plan, a roadmap, something to guide you into the unknown. That is exactly the purpose of this book, to provide you with a place to start and target at which to shoot. There is a Confucius saying, *"Man who aim at nothing is sure to hit it!"* I'm looking to put it all into perspective for you and supply a little direction.

- If you have not yet started to build your online store, this is the absolute perfect time for you to be reading this book. It will prevent you from making mistakes that could cost you hundreds of hours and thousands of dollars. You will know more about what lies ahead before you take the leap and start building your site.

- If your online boutique is less than a year old, this book will tell you how to improve it. You'll learn more about marketing tactics and how to increase both traffic and sales. Year one is the "get your feet wet" period. Akin to a college freshman, the first 12 months is usually spent figuring out what to do, how to do it, making some mistakes, and hoping to not wake up with a colossal hangover. But never fear, if you have already developed the headache, I'm here to provide some much-needed aspirin and a big glass of water!

- If you have been online for a year or more, I'll take you back to the basics and introduce some ideas that will make sense for you now. Often, when we first begin, there are many meaningful projects that we know would benefit our business, we just don't have time to do them as the energy is focused on the launch more than the long-term development. Now might be the perfect time to fine-tune, refocus, and implement strategies that can take you to the next level and improve profits.

Whether you already have an online dog boutique, are in the process of building one, or are simply curious about getting started, I promise that you will benefit from reading what I have to say. I don't hold anything back here and it is simple enough for even the complete internet rookie. So read on…

Ok everybody, listen up!

There are two routes that you can take when getting this production off the ground. Route one is the Hobby Plan. Now, the Hobby

Plan is fun and you can have a really neat website and impress all of your friends and family members. After the site is active, you won't really need to do too much, learn too much, or work too much. But the trade off is that you will spend more money than you make. Yes, you'll be a business owner and get some tax benefits and have a fancy business card with your name and web address on it, but your website will drain your bank account rather than add to it.

The second route is the Business Builder Plan. This route will require you to focus and learn some things that you have never before done. It will require you to pay close attention to details. It will require you to learn how to do some basic yet important work on your website (you can hire someone to do all the tough designing but you'll end up paying a fortune if you need to outsource all of your day-to-day updates and changes). It will require you to develop some online marketing skills, handle customer service issues, and have an extreme amount of persistence and determination. I'll warn you right now that if you think that this route will be quick and easy, you are in for a big surprise. However, all that being said, the Business Builder Plan is actually where you can make some money and that is the goal, right? As a Business Builder, you may need to change your mindset. If this is your first shot at entrepreneurialism, then you may be in for a shock. Plan on some late nights at the computer for a while, especially if you are still working a full-time job, and there will be plenty of obstacles and frustrations. There's a saying that I love, *"To err is human, but to really screw things up it takes a computer!"* I remember a few years back when one day my computer just decided to go on strike. I've got the phone ringing, orders to fill, postage and invoices to print... and no computer. A memorable day without a doubt, one I'd love to forget. Trust me, things like this **will** happen to you from time to time. Nothing you can do but accept it and keep moving forward, so prepare your brain for it now and when it does happen you'll be able to cope a bit better.

Although the Hobby Plan people will find this book helpful and informative, it is the Business Builders for whom this book is intended. I want to help you make money and do it faster than you could do it on your own. My approach to this book is that I am the CEO of my company and I am talking to another company CEO... and that's YOU! I am not here to lecture you, but rather help you by sharing my experiences. You are now a business owner, you are the CEO, you are the decision maker. Success or failure is now up to YOU! Time to look in the mirror and introduce yourself to the boss!

Finally, before I get down to the nuts and bolts, I want to touch on two key qualities that I believe are imperative for any entrepreneur- *Initiative* and *Awareness*. When you are an employee, you can often just show up for work, do the required task for the day, collect a paycheck, and go home. As an entrepreneur, showing up for work may mean getting out of bed and walking to the computer. The required task for the day is not defined until **you** actually define it. There is no boss to tell you what needs to be done, you need to figure that out on your own. Then, of course, there is also no paycheck. Yes, there may be profits, but they are definitely not a paycheck and should not be treated the same way. The investment of time and money into your business is an ongoing process. The *initiative* is your responsibility and you must hold yourself accountable to take it each and every day (yes, that means nights and weekends, especially in the beginning). *Awareness* refers to being aware of your surroundings, your contacts, your experiences, and your opportunities. As an employee, you can put the blinders on, go hibernate, and do your job. Now that you are an entrepreneur, you must have keen senses, carefully evaluate every opportunity, and learn how to direct your own ship. If you do not pay attention, you could miss the perfect shot at something big. Successful entrepreneurs have the *awareness* to recognize an opportunity and the *initiative* to take action.

. . .

Why is This Book Different?

A legitimate question indeed- one that I would be more than happy to answer.

If you are looking for a book that will explain how to build an online store from A to Z, there are dozens of literary options. You could easily fill a bookcase with books published on the topic in the last 2-3 years. I've read many of them, some good and some bad, and here's a short list of things that I wanted to improve upon:

- *Too technical-* Most online dog boutique owners are pursuing their initial internet venture. I know from experience that it can be overwhelming, confusing, frustrating, etc... You need a book that tempers those feelings rather than fosters them.

- *Too General-* The typical author is writing his/her book with no knowledge of the dog industry and does not know the struggles and needs of the niche. My background and experience working with dog boutique owners, combined with the fact that I *am* a dog boutique owner gives me more insight into your needs.

- *Too Sneaky-* I was surprised and shocked when I realized that so many of these "how to" books really should have been titled, *"How to Read My Book and Then Buy More of My Stuff!"* The primary focus of seemed to be pushing additional products and services. Yes, I will give my company a few shameless plugs throughout this publication, but my focus is to help your website become more profitable. Tools and companies that I recommend to you here are a result of my positive experiences, not my income.

- *Not Enough Marketing Help-* A book that explains how to build an eCommerce site but fails to provide adequate instruction on marketing trains you to spend money rather than make money. In my opinion, the marketing section needs to be bigger than the technical section. You want your website to be a profit center, not a money pit!

- *Too Outdated-* With many industries, reading content or advice that was written 18-24 months ago would be no big deal as things tend not to change too much in a short period of time. Unfortunately, the internet doesn't work that way. In a brief year or two, light-years of transition can occur online. Search engines change their rules, advertising techniques are upgraded and improved, new innovations appear which make last year's stuff obsolete. 2009 may not seem that long ago, but if you are getting marketing advice from a book published back then, you'll be missing out on too much information.

Eventually I will look to publish a more in-depth version of my *"Blueprint for Building an Online Dog Boutique"* but for now, this is what you really need to know fashioned in a way as to not add more confusion and overload.

• • •

Business License/Tax ID Number/Resale Permit/ Tax Write-Offs

Let's get this one out of the way right up front. One thing that I will not do during the course of this book or any other time is offer legal, tax, accounting, or financial advice. For these matters, I suggest you contact the properly licensed professionals or an appropriate government agency. Laws will differ from state to state so you should do your homework and make sure that everything is done correctly and within the law. This book will provide accurate and authoritative information based on my personal experiences as well as experiences from others in the industry. Keep in mind that technology is ever changing and although every attempt is being made to provide you with the most current information, there will always be changing circumstances that are beyond our control.

• • •

Designing Your Website

With regards to getting your website up and running, it is interesting that most internet newbies will assume that web design and construction is the most important aspect of starting an online dog boutique. Obviously a significant step, but as I will discuss later, it really is not the most critical part of your business. I also will not discuss finding suppliers and products. Believe it or not, that task is easy compared to some of the other work you have ahead of you. Spend a few hours on Google and you can find more suppliers than you can handle. Contact them, ask a few questions, set up accounts with the ones you like, and you are well on your way. But as long as I'm touching on the topic, I'll throw in a cheap plug for my company, Doggie Designer (www.doggiedesigner.net). We dropship for hundreds of sites and have been doing so successfully for years. Make sure you set up an account with us! The one piece of advice I will offer here is that you want to make sure you are dealing with companies that are easy to reach and responsive. Too often, if you are working with a dropshipper overseas, there will be severe challenges with communication and service. When there is a problem, your customer will not care who is at fault, they will blame you and your reputation will be tarnished. Put a call into the supplier before signing up with them and get a feeling for their support staff. If you are still working a full-time job, you may want to look for suppliers who will answer the phone before or after your work hours and on weekends.

I have a few pretty strong opinions about getting your website set up. You can agree or disagree with me but my opinions are based on years of watching people run into some major problems. There are plenty of companies online that will build a website for you. Some are good and some are bad, but most will charge quite a bit of money. I have seen new boutique "hopefuls" spend $10,000+ on getting their site developed and end up in a nightmare situation where the money is gone and the site is still not operational. Rather than drone on and on about the massive list of fiascos I've witnessed, let's suffice it to say that you really need to know who you are dealing with and these companies that are out there building websites for masses of people really do not care if you ever make any money. They definitely care about their own profits, but not too much about yours. Usually, they have no experience in the pet industry and they do not always know how to build a site that is marketable online. I'll get more into this topic later but in a nutshell, web design and web marketing are two completely different animals. 99% of the time, good web designers are horrible web marketers (the opposite is also usually true) and if your site is not built with the proper keywords and on-site optimization from the start, then you will have a very difficult time ranking well with the search engines and you may end up re-designing parts of your site down the road- a frustrating, time consuming, and costly assignment. How do you prevent this? Well, the upcoming chapters of this book will teach you some important aspects of website optimization so you can have that discussion with your web designers before you pay them. My company builds great websites for people for about $2000 so I think it's silly to pay more than that.

Keep in mind that even if you have someone else build your website for you, there will still be ongoing updates, changes, product/inventory fluctuations, and other events that will make website maintenance a regular occurrence. If you do not build the site yourself, make sure the company that designs your site teaches you how to perform these maintenance issues. The last thing you want is to have to pay someone every time your site needs a minor update. Web designers can command a hefty hourly rate and will eat into your profits handsomely. I am not suggesting that you design the site on your own, as that is a monumental task, but at the very least be competent enough to add/delete products, change pricing and descriptions, make minor text changes, and add/delete images. These are rudimentary skills that anyone planning on surviving online must master.

• • •

Hosting Companies

If you are new to this, then you probably do not understand hosting companies and their function. However, they are perhaps one of the most important factors when building your site. This topic can get confusing, so let's see if I can simplify this for you…

A hosting company provides the platform for your website. They provide space on what is called a *server* which allows your site to be accessible on the World Wide Web. There are different types of hosting companies that specialize in different types of websites. Some are great for blogs or personal web pages and others are better suited for eCommerce sites such as your boutique. (eCommerce refers to the fact that you will be selling items directly through a shopping cart on your site.) They will range in price from $6.95 to $100+ per month and will also have different programs and features. Please do not pick a hosting company based solely on price or you may have trouble down the road. Here are a few things to consider when choosing a hosting company.

- If you have a site built on a server and the hosting company goes out of business, you lose your site and you must start over from scratch (I've seen it happen and it is a nightmare).

- If you ever decide to change hosting companies in the future, you will lose not only your site, but any *search engine rankings* that you have earned with that site. This actually happened to my company and is the reason why we now have two sites- .com and .net. It can be confusing for customers so you want to avoid it if possible. Here's one of those times when you can learn from our mistake. There will be plenty more opportunities like this!

- Free or inexpensive hosting companies and plans may have restrictions that impair your business, such as limiting the number of pages/products on your site or limiting the amount of bandwidth you can use. These hosting plans are great for blogs and smaller sites, but not for a complex eCommerce site with a shopping cart.

Bandwidth refers to the amount of data transfer that occurs across your site.

Ok, I can see that your eyes are starting to glaze over so if necessary, stop, take a deep breath, reread the last few paragraphs and then continue with a clear brain.

Whew, now let's discuss bandwidth...

Think of bandwidth like memory. The more people that go to your site and the more pages they look at, the more bandwidth gets used. Now, think about this for a second. You have an online store, the goal is to get **lots** of people to go there, spend **lots** of time there, and come back over and over again. With that in mind, would you want to choose a hosting company that limits your bandwidth or charges you for it? In my opinion, for what it's worth, that is the last thing you would want to do.

Some hosting companies will start you with a low monthly fee but then charge you extra after you use a certain amount of bandwidth. Other companies will charge a higher fixed monthly fee and give you unlimited bandwidth. Still others will provide free bandwidth but take a small percentage of the sales that go through your site. There is no right or wrong here, you just must decide what is best for the long term goals of your company. Remember, you are the CEO and as CEO, you need to see the big picture here and take the proper course of action.

• • •

How Does Google Work?

Throughout this book, I'm going to make numerous references to Google. I do this because they are obviously the leader and most widely used search engine. However, it is important for you to know that the rules are generally the same for all of the search engines. Although slight variances may exist, if you make Google happy, you will make everyone happy, and in order to have any shot whatsoever at satisfying Google, then you must learn their rules and what it is that they want. Here are the major factors that influence Google's rankings (at the time of publication):

- Relevancy
- Popularity
- Original Content
- "Buzz"

Let me explain each one of these concepts.

Relevancy

A simple way to think about relevancy is this, "Does the content of your page match the keywords that you are targeting?" You may or may not know this, but when your site is designed, every page of your website has its own keywords and descriptions typed into the code. It is not visible, but it's there. You literally can give any description and assign any keywords to each page. The conflict comes about when your keywords and descriptions do not match the content of the page. Here's an example:

> *I was asked by an online boutique owner if I would look at her site and give her suggestions on how she might be able to improve her rankings. She had been in business for 6-8*

months and was getting very little traffic and very few sales. Frustrated, she did the right thing and asked for help. I logged on to her site and immediately saw an obvious problem. She was attempting to rank her home page for about 10 different keyword phrases all with the word "dog" in them (things like "fancy dog clothes" and "designer dog accessories"), but the word "dog" appeared **nowhere** on the page. I truly am not exaggerating when I say that "dog" was not written anywhere on her home page. Yes, she had a few nice pictures of dogs wearing beautiful outfits, but since Google can't see pictures, they were not helping her rankings. How do you think Google viewed her relevancy? She was using "dog" keywords in her code but her page made no mention of dogs. Remember a few pages back when I said that website designers are usually poor website marketers? Well, here's the perfect example of an attractive website that is perfectly worthless. Google will never find her unless some serious changes are made and if she doesn't know how to make these changes herself, then she'll have to go back and pay someone to do it. In my opinion, a decent web designer should have avoided this problem. What should she have done? Well, if she is trying to rank her home page for "fancy dog clothes" then she really needs to have that exact phrase written 1-2 times somewhere on the home page. It could be a category or maybe worked into the description of a product, but it needs to be there. That alone will not result in high rankings but on-page factors such as this are critical.

Popularity

Popularity online has nothing to do with how "cool" you are or how many people like you. Rather, popularity refers to the number of sites that are linked to you and how popular *those* sites are. What you will find is that websites appearing high in the search engine rankings usually have hundreds or even thousands of inbound links to their site. When Google sees all of these links, they interpret that as *popularity* and it helps rankings. Links from high quality authority sites carry more weight with Google than links from new sites or blank directories. This means that a link on YouTube that leads to your home page is more significant than a link on your best friend's blog. The best situation is having *relevant* links from *relevant* sites. I'll discuss good and bad links later in the marketing section.

Original Content

This may sound like common sense but you never want to copy too much of someone else's content. For instance, you go to a popular online boutique site that happens to rank well for the keywords you want. With some weird logic you decide that since their site ranks so well, you'll just copy everything they have done verbatim. Bad idea... Your site will fail miserably so don't bother. Take the time to do things right and create your own content. Taking shortcuts online rarely ever works and definitely not in this case.

Buzz

Buzz refers to the activity that is created as you develop original, relevant content on your site and then take the necessary steps to build popularity. This means you will need to take an active role in promoting your site, especially in the beginning when no one even knows that you exist. Plan on exploring other sites to create links to yours, posting content on blogs and forums, learning how to utilize social bookmarking, and doing other things to get noticed. There are literally hundreds of activities and skills you can learn that will manifest this buzz. The key is consistently taking action over a prolonged period of time. You are now a business owner, get out there and promote your business!

• • •

On-Site Optimization

Wikipedia defines search engine optimization as "the process of improving the visibility of a website or a web page in search engines via the natural or un-paid ("organic" or "algorithmic") search results". In Southern California, we would just say "Doing stuff to your website to make it come up higher in Google, Dude." When you are "doing this stuff" on the web pages themselves, it is referred to as "on-site" or "on-page" optimization. I want to avoid confusion and complication with this book, which is not an easy thing to do when your topic is the internet, so I just want to discuss three simple strategies that you can use on your site to improve your chances of ranking well.

• • •

Keyword Density

Although there is some debate among the gurus when it comes to keyword density, the general consensus is that the keywords for any one page should appear at a frequency of roughly 3%. Let's look at an example to help this make sense.

> Assume that one of the keyword phrases you are targeting on a page is "leather dog collars" and that page has roughly 200 words on it. 3% of 200 is six words. Since "leather dog collars" is 3 words, then you would want that phrase to appear twice on the page. Now, is it a big deal if the phrase is written only once or maybe even three times? No, not at all. The 3% is just a guideline, not a rule.

Take a look at each page on your site. Examine the keywords being used and how often they materialize on the page.

• • •

Categories

One easy way to incorporate your targeted keywords into your site is to use keywords as your category titles whenever possible. For instance, if you are optimizing your home page for the term "fancy dog sweaters", then consider having a category with that name appear on the page. You'll not only be improving keyword density but also generating a link within your site that uses "fancy dog sweaters" as anchor text. (This will make more sense after you read the chapter on keywords and anchor text in the marketing section.)

• • •

Permalinks

Permalinks normally refer to blog pages but depending upon your hosting company and the flexibility within your web platform, there is some value in discussing it here. This probably falls under an advanced classification so consider it to be optional for now.

Consider this url for one of my web pages:
http://www.doggiedesigner.net/handmade_leather_dog_collars. html

In this web address, the permalink is *handmade_leather_dog_collars* and with most websites, you have the ability to change the permalink to the word or words of your choice. If this is the case with your site, then why not make sure that whenever possible, your permalink matches one of your keywords? Remember, one of the factors examined by Google is relevancy. Matching your permalinks to your keywords makes the page more relevant and improves your odds of getting to that coveted page one. Does it really work? Well, I can tell you that only 1 month after creating the page on our website, it ranked #21 out of over 46,000 results for the search terms "handmade leather dog collars". Not bad.

. . .

Credit Cards/Paypal

No need to spend a ton of time on this topic, but I believe you should be accepting as many forms of payment as you possibly can. If you want to process credit cards through your site, you will need to contact either your bank or another reputable financial institution and get details on setting up a *merchant services account* (that's the fancy term for accepting credit cards). Let them know that your business is online and they will tell you what you need to know. This process can take a few weeks to get up and running so do not wait until the last minute. You may also want to check out more than one bank and compare fees. A word to the wise here... there are so many independent merchant services companies out there and they will all try to convince you that they have the lowest fees or rates. Unfortunately, there are too many places where seemingly innocent charges can be slipped in and you never even know about them. My advice is to pick a bank or financial institution that is well known rather than a company you have never heard of with a slick talking sales person on the other end of the phone. But, that being said, you are the CEO so it is up to you. One other detail to consider is that most banks/merchant services companies will require a 2-5 year term commitment with penalties as high as $500 for early termination. Make sure you are comfortable with this before you sign your name on the dotted line.

A merchant services account through your bank will get you started with VISA, MasterCard, and Discover, but American Express is an entirely different animal. If you want to accept AmEx, and I would definitely recommend it, you will need to contact them directly. They process their own accounts independently of the others. You can research them and obtain further information online at www. americanexpress.com.

I do feel that it is mandatory for you to accept Paypal these days. Too many people are uncomfortable using credit cards online (and for good reason) so you must have a Paypal account set up. Doing this is a simple process, go to www.paypal.com and register for a new account if you do not already have one. Your hosting company will help you to integrate your merchant services and Paypal accounts with your eCommerce shopping cart.

• • •

Pictures and Product Descriptions

Make sure that your hosting company supports high resolution pictures and displays them in a way that they are big and impressive enough on your site to capture and hold the reader's attention. Some of the less expensive hosting companies will limit the size of your photographs. Others may limit the number of products that you can list on your site. Neither situation is particularly advantageous for you. If you want to have the best opportunity for success, then you really want to make sure that your pictures and your product descriptions are top notch. It is worth the extra time to get them done right. Many companies will offer you the ability to use their images and descriptions. If the images are not high quality, then I would think twice before adding them to your site. If the descriptions are not detailed enough, then you may want to rewrite them yourself. Sites that permit the visitor to click on the photos and enlarge them are particularly effective and useful as they allow better detail and are more user-friendly.

. . .

Writing and Text

This is a good spot to talk about the text on your site. What I'm talking about here are your product descriptions, your policies/ procedures, your "About Us" page (which you absolutely must have), and any other pages on your site that contain text. Nothing will chase away a potential customer faster than grammatical or spelling errors. These simple little mistakes are amateur and cannot be tolerated by a competent CEO such as yourself. If you are a proficient writer, you can compose these pages yourself. If you find the writing process to be challenging, that's ok, just hire someone to do it for you or solicit the help of a friend who might have some skills in this area. After the text is posted, proofread it for errors and have someone else do the same. Too often, if we write the text ourselves, it is easy to miss our own mistakes. This is a very competitive industry and you do not want to lose customers because of typos that could have been corrected.

With regards to an "About Us" page, make sure you spend some time developing this. Many savvy customers will read this page before they place an order. They'll want to know who you are, where you are, and a bit of background to make them feel more secure in their purchase. I suggest having a picture or two on this page and you might even consider adding a brief introductory video here. I'll talk more about videos later in the book but for now, what I want you to think about is the most basic concept of running a successful business, "People will do business with people they like." The more you can make them like you, the better your chances are of getting their order. Aside from all of this, there is another critical reason why you must have a respectable "About Us" page. Google will often penalize you if you don't. A manual review of your site can occur at any time, and if it does, your rankings will severely suffer if you are missing an "About Us" page. For the same reasons, your site will also require a "Contact Us" link or page. The bottom line is that the search engines want to protect their users. One way for them to accomplish this is to lower the rankings of sites that are published anonymously. Make sure that you are not in this category.

• • •

Returns and Shipping Policies

If you are dealing with more than one supplier, and you most likely will be, then you are also going to have to deal with different return policies and shipping rates for each supplier. Don't make this any tougher for yourself than necessary. Simply make your policies and rates equal to those of your most stringent supplier. For instance, if one supplier charges a 10% restocking fee for returns and another charges 20%, then make your policy 20% for all returns. You break even with your toughest supplier and make a little extra for your time and effort on the others. You should NEVER lose money on an exchange. I'll say it again, you are the CEO and you are responsible for making policies that benefit your company. Take the same strategic approach when you set your shipping rates.

If you strictly adhere to dropshipping, you will not need to worry about selecting a postal carrier since your supplier will be doing all the shipping. However, if you plan on stocking a small inventory, you will need to deal with packing and shipping. When choosing your shipping methods, my best advice is talk to account representatives with UPS and FedEx and then compare with the US Postal Service (for US based business owners). If you are outside the US, talk to your local postal carrier. Honestly, until you start moving a large number of packages each month, there really will not be much difference, at least not enough to spend a great deal of time worrying about it. But if your volume increases, make sure you have a plan for this.

• • •

Adding Video to Your Site

When selecting a hosting company or website template, make sure that you have the option to add videos to your web pages. I cannot stress to you enough what a huge difference a few very simple videos will make on your site. Let me tell you a quick story. In our efforts to enhance the Doggie Designer product line, we are always on the lookout for unique merchandise with good profit margins. In the summer of 2009 we added an innovative little product to our website, a car safety belt that keeps your dog from jumping all over the car while you drive. It is incredibly easy to use, low cost, and it protects both the dog and the owner. For only $15 retail, it really was one of the smartest items on our entire site. People that purchased the belts loved them and although we literally sold hundreds of them in our retail store, we couldn't seem to have the same results online. After months of wondering why this was happening, it struck me that in the store we would provide a brief, 15 second demonstration with the belt and that little demo gave us a closing rate of approximately 60-70% with everyone who saw it. On the website, however, there was no demonstration! I did a little bit of research and found out that I could add video to my product descriptions online, so I bought an inexpensive hand held video camera (very easy to use) and recorded a 90 second video of myself demonstrating the car safety belt. The results were dramatic. Within just a matter of a few days our online sales (both retail and wholesale) started to pick up and we now sell dozens of belts each month from our website. If you've seen the video, you will notice that it is nothing special or fancy and it took less than 10 minutes to film, but by simply adding this personal touch to the site, we improved our revenue about $350 per month. Hmmm... an easy to use video camera for $150 and 90 seconds of video results in an extra $4200 per year. Time for you to make another one of those CEO decisions! Small additions like this provide you with an edge over the dozens of other online dog boutiques that do not bother with such details. In the ultra competitive online shopping world, seemingly insignificant alterations often make dramatic differences.

MARKETING YOUR SITE

We've Only Just Begun

I guess I could be dating myself by using a reference to an old Carpenters tune, but I'm a sucker for the oldies. Sorry! Well, the previous section on getting your website started was the appetizer and now we are moving on to the main course. (Hmm… the Carpenters followed by a food suggestion, kind of like being on a first date in the 70's.) Seriously, even though the process of launching your site may seem like the ultimate goal, it is not the culmination of your work, but rather the commencement of it. Yes, if you thought that you spent a ton of time and effort putting your site together and getting it to look just right, your real time investment has only just begun. It would be impossible for me to cover all the potential marketing strategies and teach you proficiency within the pages of this book. Instead, I will discuss some of the more popular methods and give you enough pertinent details for you to decide which methods appeal to you most. Once you make that determination, learn all you can about those techniques and get to work. Here's a word of caution. Online boutique owners will get what is often referred to as "paralysis of analysis" which is to say that they refrain from performing simple marketing efforts as they spend hours and hours reading, researching, and trying to learn everything before they start the marketing campaign. If I can stress any one thing it would be to take action. I know that you may not fully understand the entire course of action, but by simply "doing" you will learn, adapt, change, improve, and perfect. Marketing is an ongoing process that will never truly end. Think about this for a second, if giant mega-stores such as Target and Wal-Mart realize the importance of consistent marketing even though they have household names, wouldn't it stand to reason that you, as a small business owner, should make an effort which is just as steady? Yes, of course it will be at a tiny fraction of the budget, but this fixed endeavor is actually more important for you than it is for the big boys.

Sadly, it is this aspect of online business ownership where I see the greatest number of people fail. If you are like most website owners, this is probably your first venture into entrepreneurialism and definitely your initial internet enterprise. That means you may have quite a bit to learn about online marketing and driving traffic to your website. Since your desire is to realize a profit, you really have only two choices here:

- Learn how to market your site, or

- Pay someone else to market your site

Option number one will cost you a little bit of money and a significant amount of time while option number two will cost you a little bit of time and a significant amount of money. Those with a good sized budget ($1500-4000 per month or more), can literally pay to acquire traffic and customers. If you are operating on a limited budget, which most people are when they get started, then you better face the reality that you will need to learn a few online skills that you have never done before. Being a computer expert is definitely NOT necessary, but being open and willing to develop some online competence is a must. The one deadly combination here is the lack of a budget for paid marketing and the lack of time and patience to learn self promotion online.

It may surprise you to find out how many resourceful ways there are to promote your website absolutely free or for a very small fee. In fact, some of the secrets that I will share with you in the upcoming pages are strategies that the companies promising to "Get you to the top of Google" do not want you to know. Why? Because they love charging you hundreds of dollars each month for work that you could easily do yourself for free. Or, at the very least, if you understood exactly what you needed to do, you could most likely find someone that would do it at a lower price. Here's a lesson that you can learn from one of my many mistakes...

When I first started online, I hired a company to "optimize" my site and improve my rankings. Let's just call them the *XYZ Company*. The guy on the other end of the phone sounded pretty convincing and somewhat educated, so I agreed to pay him $300 per month for this service. What, exactly, were they going to do for me? Heck, I didn't really know, but everyone out there says that you need to "optimize" your site and since I had no clue of how to "optimize" the logical decision was that I should pay someone to do it for me. Thus, the credit card charges of $300 every month began! After 90 days, when my rankings were not any better, I asked if this was normal. "Yes, it is absolutely normal," replied Chuck, my personal customer relations assistant with *XYZ*. "It can take 6-7 months before we actually see the results we want, but we are certain that we can get you to page one for the keywords we are targeting." Ok, I didn't know any better so I waited and waited. Three more months and $900 more dollars went by with no change in the rankings. I called Chuck again, who assured me that we were on the right path. Completely confused, I threw another 3 months and another $900 at this and after month nine, I was no better off than I was at month one! Now I'm out $2700 and feeling completely exploited. (Is any of this starting to sound familiar? I know this has happened to a lot of website owners.) I asked Chuck to explain what specific service they were providing for $300 that should be granting me these coveted high rankings. Simply put, he told me that his company had access to hundreds of websites and that they were putting links to my site out there in cyberland. These links would, in time, improve my rankings. Well, tired of paying the $300 I cancelled my service with XYZ and decided that I needed to learn more about "optimizing" and this process of link building before I racked up any more charges on my credit card.

Chuck was telling me the truth about a few things, namely, that the links (sometimes called backlinks) would help my site to improve in the rankings. However, he failed to tell me a few other things about backlinks that were relatively important, one being that I could actually build these links on my own for FREE! Hmmm... $2700 spent over nine months for something that I could have done for free in less than half the time. I was not a happy camper but guys, here's a universal truth that you need to understand right now.

If you are uninformed or uneducated about something, you will always end up paying someone who IS informed and educated.

I was flat out uninformed and uneducated when it came to "optimizing" so I was forced to pay for my ignorance. I only wish I could have paid less for the lesson. Right then and there I made the decision to wise up, get educated, and learn how to market my site online so I would never get stuck in this trap again. Plus, I figured that any knowledge I could pick up would be strategies I could then pass on to others. It was a win-win and I absolutely needed to start immediately.

• • •

Your Domain Name

Keeping in mind the fact that the first goal is for customers to be able to easily find you online, you will want to give some serious thought to your domain name (www.yourdomainname.com). Enticing as it might be to brainstorm a clever and witty name for your website, most often you will be better served by selecting a domain that is closely related to terms for which someone might search when looking for your product line. An absolutely perfect example of this is a company called Small Pet Clothes, www.smallpetclothes.com. What their name lacks in ingenuity is more than compensated with functionality. Out of 13,000,000 sites that rank for the keywords "small pet clothes", they are number one based primarily on their dead-on domain name. That's basically FREE advertising and FREE web traffic due to extremely wise name selection. It may not sound as fun as "Puffy's Puppy Paradise" but as a new website owner, put your ego aside and sacrifice cute in exchange for customers.

Another quick tip on domain selection- settle only for a .com or a .net site. Ideally, you want the .com and only if you have exhausted every possible .com should you then move on to .net.

The .com will nearly always outrank a .net. My company owns both www.doggiedesigner.com and www.doggiedesigner.net and the .com ranks higher in almost every search. Why? The search engines like .com's better. Granted, you might find a few "guru's" who will argue this point, but try a little research study of your own by searching for *anything.* Any search, any search engine, any search terms and what do you see on page one? Nine out of ten on page one and maybe even ten out of ten are all .com's. That's enough proof for me.

. . .

Keywords and Keyword Research

Keywords make the world (wide web) go round! Everything online is driven by keywords. When you go to one of the search engines and type in search terms, you are typing keywords. When Google finds you, they find you by using keywords. When you have your site optimized, you are optimizing for specific keywords (even if you do not know it). As a matter of fact, there is nothing more important to your survival online than keywords. Now, just to eliminate any potential confusion, I want to differentiate between a keyword and a keyword phrase. If you perform an internet search for "restaurant", then "restaurant" is a keyword. But, do the exact same search for "Italian restaurant" and now you are using a *keyword phrase* only because it is more than one word. Got it? Good, let's move on and continue with this example by discussing *anchor text.*

I know that you are familiar with anchor text even though you may not realize it. Assume that you are reading an online article and you come across the words "Italian restaurant" and they are underlined and in a different color font. You know immediately that this is a link that you can click and when you do, it will take you to another page, presumably a page where you will find an Italian restaurant or more information about one. In this case, "Italian restaurant" is a keyword phrase being used as <u>anchor text</u> leading to a second site. If you owned an Italian restaurant and wanted your business to rank highly for this search term, it is exactly the type of link you would want. The more of these anchor text links you have, the better you will rank for that keyword phrase. Capisce?

There are resources that you can use online to identify keywords and phrases within you specific business niche. A popular one is Google's Keyword Tool. It is free to use and you can find it quickly just by Googling the phrase "keyword tool". It will give you great information such as the number of monthly searches performed for any given search term as well as the amount of competition that exists for that term. A wise website owner will always try to target specific keywords within his/her niche, but an extremely wise website owner will try to target keywords that have lower competition. Listen, any type of marketing is a war. You are competing against every other company or site out there trying to sell the same or similar product line. So if you are going to war, do you want to fight a bunch of big guys that really know how to fight or a bunch of little guys who haven't really learned how to punch yet. For me, I don't like to get beat up so I pick the little guys and try to attack them. Once you successfully accomplish this a few times, you might find that you are actually challenging a few of the bigger boys and giving them a run for their money. Soon thereafter, you will be one of the big boys! Here's a contrasting example...

> *Marge is a new online dog boutique owner and she is look-*
> *ing to optimize her site. She assumes that she needs to*

optimize for keywords such as "dog clothes", "dog collars", "dog leashes", and "dog accessories". She starts down that road by making the proper changes to her site and building links with anchor text using these keyword phrases. Unknowingly, she has chosen keywords with extremely high competition. In fact, she is fighting well experienced sites with potentially hundreds of thousands of backlinks and anchor text for these keywords. Needless to say, Marge never cracks higher than page 6 or 7 for any of these terms.

Shirley is also a new online boutique owner. Before starting her optimizing efforts, she does some research and finds keywords that have much less competition. These phrases are a bit longer such as "custom leather dog collars" and "designer clothes for Yorkies". She begins optimizing, creating backlinks and anchor text using these keyword phrases and within a few months, she finds herself on page one for these terms!

Now, let's talk about Marge and Shirley and their approaches. Marge was right about wanting to use those pertinent keywords for her site. But, she picked a fight with the big boys and they kicked her butt! Shirley, on the other hand, knows that her keywords will get far less searches, but she is willing to sacrifice those numbers in exchange for winning the fight. Even though Shirley's keywords might get only 1000 searches per month versus Marge's 1,000,000, Shirley still wins because she gets traffic from the 1000 while Marge gets nothing from the 1,000,000. How did Shirley accomplish this? She used the Keyword Tool and put in a few hours of research to find keywords in her niche with lower competition.

This is an extremely critical concept for you to understand and it helps if you comprehend it before you build your site. If you do, then you can incorporate the right keywords into your pages when you build them. Otherwise, you may have to go back and make changes to your site once it is done to make sure you are using keywords that make the most sense. In my humble opinion, this fact right here is the exact reason why you should use a web designer that has some experience in the dog industry. They really need to have the proper keyword factors in place for you and too often new boutique owners never consider this when having their sites built. The result? A site that is really difficult for your target audience to find and this means very few sales.

• • •

Good and Bad Links

Now that you understand keywords, keyword phrases, anchor text, and backlinks, we need to discuss right and wrong ways of creating backlinks to your site. Knowing how to do this correctly can have a tremendous impact on your site's visibility, but conversely, doing this incorrectly can cause a myriad of problems. Too many improper backlinks can actually result in your site being banned by Google. Don't panic, it is highly doubtful that you are anywhere near having an overabundance of bad links, but you need to know that this risk exists out there.

Stop for a second and try to think like a search engine. What is their main objective? They want to provide accurate and pertinent information to their customers. When someone searches for "car insurance quotes", the engine identifies websites that have the biggest web presence built around those keywords. It looks for the most popular sites in this category based on content, links, visitors, etc… It also factors in whether or not this popularity occurred naturally (organically) or if it was forced or manipulated somehow. For example, a site that has been in existence for years and over that time has accumulated thousands of links and traffic due to visitors going to the site and then linking to it will rank highly with Google. On the other end of the spectrum, consider a brand new site that had very few links last week but suddenly has 10,000 links today. Although it is possible for this to happen naturally if your site is an overnight sensation, the reality is that it just is not normal for 10,000 links to appear within a week, or even a month, if a site is new. Google's "spiders" have a way of detecting this and it is viewed as an attempt to trick the search engines and often will result in the site being banned forever. Remember, Google wants to protect its customers so they aren't interested in passing this type of site on to their users. The bottom line here is that you do want thousands of links leading back to your site, but you want those links to occur over time and you want the correct types of links.

Types of Links

The easiest way to understand good vs. bad links is for me to define them.

- One-way links
- Two-way links
- Three-way links

• • •

One-Way Links

The search engines love these! Why? Because they are the most natural form of links and they primarily occur when people approve of your site and its content. An example of a one-way link would be someone who visits your site, loves it, and then bookmarks it on a site such as Digg, Delicious, or StumbleUpon. Social bookmarking sites like these allow people to save their favorite sites in one spot and share the list with others. You absolutely want as many social bookmarks as possible. You must have a social bookmarking "widget" built in to your site. It simplifies the process, making it easy for someone to bookmark one of your pages. If you do not already have this feature on your site, I'm sure you have seen it elsewhere. But, just in case, here's how it works. Built in to your webpages are icons or links to the most popular social bookmarking sites. If, while net surfing, the reader sees something they appreciate, they click the proper icon and the page is automatically stored for them to be able to easily find it again later. Check out an example by going to my site, http://www.doggiedesigner.net, and you'll see the "share" icon at the top of the home page. Feel free to bookmark it while you are there!

Another example of a one-way link would be a blog or forum post where someone discusses your site and inserts a link to it. This can occur on personal blog pages or on sites such as Squidoo. Hint… a link from a highly popular site is worth more to you than a link from a site that doesn't get much traffic. You can build these links yourself by visiting any forum or blog, posting a comment, and including a link to your site. I would encourage you to do this as often as possible. Just make sure that you are contributing a comment that adds value to the forum or blog. If your comment is just a meaningless sentence or two, the moderator of the forum/blog is likely to trash your comment and your link. However, if you provide useful and stimulating content, your link will most often remain there forever. That's a free link. Score!

A few other powerful sources of one-way links are articles, videos, and press releases. All of these will be discussed in detail in the upcoming pages. What you need to know is that you can develop thousands of one-way links on your own for **free** and the absolute best thing you can do for your business is to invest your time creating as many as you possibly can.

• • •

Two-Way Links

This is commonly referred to as a link exchange and I'm sure you are familiar with it. In a nutshell, you add a link to someone's site and they add a link to yours. On the surface this sounds like a great idea, but the problem here is that Google and the other search engines have become wise to this practice. They want links that occur naturally and this practice is not natural, it is merely the acquisition of an effortless link. If the site linking to you is not relevant to your niche, then the link is relatively useless and probably not worth the time or effort. A backlink from a site selling tires will rarely help your online pet boutique to improve rankings. That being said, if you happen to have contact with others in your niche and you decide to exchange links, even though it may not help your ranking much, it could result in some cross-over traffic that leads to sales so that situation does offer some value. A word of caution, however, is to make sure you are familiar with a site before you agree to swap links. Otherwise you could get caught in a *three-way link* and that is potential trouble you want to avoid.

• • •

Three-Way Links

These links are detrimental to your site and, unfortunately, if you are new to online marketing you could unknowingly fall into this trap. Here's the scenario, perhaps a familiar one:

> *You receive an email from a company saying something like "Dear Website Owner, we have come across your website and we are very impressed. We happen to have a similar site in the same industry as yours and would like to exchange links with you. We have placed a link to your home page in our directory and would appreciate if you could reciprocate by inserting our link into your site."*

Listen, I know that you have probably received dozens of these emails and if you are new, be ready because they will come. It sounds like a great deal right? A website owner comes out of nowhere and wants to put your link on his/her site. What a generous and thoughtful human being this person must be! How wonderful! NOT!

What's really going on here is a three-way link. If you agree to it, you'll be giving them a great link from your relevant site which will definitely help their rankings since they are doing it with thousands of people just like you. But rather than getting back a link from their primary site, you receive a useless link from a third site consisting of nothing but a page full of links. Soon, when Google realizes that this third site is bogus garbage, they ban the page and the link to your site is gone. Of course, it was never worth much from the start. In essence, you just provided someone with a great link and got nothing in return. You do not want to be affiliated with this type of situation because it could eventually lead to your own site being banned. True, the chances of this are low, but when you have invested so much in your venture, why risk it?

As a rule of thumb, ignore requests that you get from unknown sources offering link exchanges and focus your efforts on obtaining tons of one-way links. Do this and you will never run into a problem with any of the search engines. But if you want to have a little fun and potentially make some extra money, you can try this response to those link seekers. Reply to their email and kindly let them know that although you do not participate in link exchanges, you would be more than happy to provide them with a link on your site for a fee (you can make up the fee). I have actually received as much as $200 for adding a link to my website! What a cool deal that is- relatively free money! Life is good again! If you are fortunate enough to have this opportunity, just make sure you get paid *before* you add their link and do not put it on your home page. Remember, they are only after a link so you can put it anywhere on your site. I suggest inserting it in a spot where it will be relatively unnoticed.

• • •

Article Writing

Article writing is actually one of my favorite forms of online marketing. There are a number of reasons for this.

- You can target very specific keywords which makes it much easier to hit page one of the search engines.

- You can add high quality, one-way links in your articles using anchor text that lead back to your site. This not only draws people to your website, but also helps its rankings.

- Directories where articles are published are usually considered "high authority" sites by the search engines, meaning the search engines value the content within these directories and will place it higher than other similar web content. Backlinks from these sites also carry more weight than a typical backlink.

- Articles help to establish you as an expert within your niche. Want to be considered an authority on dog supplies? Just write and publish a half dozen or so articles on the topic and that is how you will be viewed.

- They are free!

I hate to use absolutes, but I would venture to say that nearly every successful online marketer either writes articles or has someone else write articles for them (a practice known as *Ghostwriting*). Ghostwriting is a great option for those of you who do not feel like you have the skills or the patience to sit down and write a 500-600 word article and publish it online. There are many writers out there that you can hire to compose a few articles for you. One word of caution here… You want your articles to be original, you need them to meet certain keyword standards, and they must be grammatically correct. This can be easy to accomplish when you author your own work, but can be significantly more difficult when outsourcing. If you shop for a writer based solely on price, you can probably locate a source overseas that will churn out articles for you at about $5.00 each. However, don't count on those articles being original or having keywords used properly. Hey, they may not even use English correctly! It does not make sense to pay for poor articles, no matter how cheap they are, so if you are new at this find a ghostwriter that can show you numerous samples, has a solid history of writing articles that rank well (top 5 of page one), and that you can talk to via phone. I do a fair amount of ghostwriting for people and I find that being able to have a person-to-person talk to clearly define your needs helps to prevent problems. If you do choose to go this route, expect to pay about $25-30 for a well written article of 500-600 words with 2 anchor text backlinks.

There are plenty of resources out there that will teach you the basics of article writing. This topic alone could easily fill 200 pages. For the sake of brevity, I'll refrain from attempting to teach you how to write your own articles. However, if you plan on surviving long term online and you do not have a substantial budget for advertising, article writing is really a skill that you will need to either develop or outsource. I have written hundreds of articles, the majority of which reached page one for the keywords I was targeting. This was accomplished not with formal writing training, but through practice and persistence, and as a result of repetition my talents in this area have developed and become very proficient. You can achieve the same results if you are willing to put forth the effort and time.

• • •

Blogging

"Blog" is short for "web log". Think of them as an online journal where you can write anything you want. If you read my introduction to this book, you know that blogging was one of those things that really intimidated me when I started marketing online. I'm not sure exactly why this was the case, but looking back now I suspect that it was primarily due to ignorance. People are usually fearful of the unknown and I knew absolutely *nothing* about blogging. Ironically, today I can honestly tell you that blogging has had a tremendously positive effect on my business and I only wish that I had started it sooner. One of my blogs has hundreds of subscribers and that number increases every day. I even have companies now that hire me to build and maintain their blogs. Since I learned the skill just by doing it, you can accomplish the same thing if you commit to the process. I am going to make an assumption here that you probably fall into that "fear of the unknown" category as well, because if you didn't, you would not be reading this book, you'd be thinking about authoring it. So, I am going to do my best to simplify this for you.

5 Reasons Why You Should Be Blogging...

- Blogs are free

- Blogs are more personal than online stores. They give the reader an opportunity to get to know you and they give you the opportunity to show customers how great you are! (If that is not one of your goals, it should be)

- Blogs are easy to update and maintain

- Search engines love blogs

- Blogs help you to establish a loyal group of followers, and that is the absolute key to longevity in ANY business.

Most successful online businesses these days have a blog that is linked to their eCommerce site. Your eCommerce site can be difficult and time consuming to update and you may need to know detailed html codes and perhaps even something about web design to properly maintain it. The opposite is true of blogs. They are easy to update, you do not need to know any html or anything about web design. You will most likely come across a few minor challenges the very first time you set one up, but these challenges are nothing compared to those you could hit with a static site and are much easier to overcome. Blogs allow you to post text, pictures, and video with minimal effort and you would probably be shocked to discover how many informational websites are really just fancy blogs.

Here's a step-by-step blogging strategy that I guarantee will help your business...

1. Start a blog by going to www.wordpress.com. It is simple, free, and arguably the best way to start your first blog. If your dog boutique has a name like, fancydoggyduds.com, then call your blog fancydoggydudsblog.com.

2. Spend some time playing around with the different features and templates. You'll quickly learn how to post content and even add pictures.

3. Write 5 new posts in your first week. They can be about anything that is related to your niche. Perhaps something funny that your dog did the other day, how much he likes his new collar, or even why you love a particular breed of dog. The bottom line here is the action of writing and posting. What you write and post is not as important as actually getting started.

4. Encourage people to subscribe to your blog! Encourage people to subscribe to your blog! Oh yeah... don't forget to encourage people to subscribe to your blog! This is how you start building a marketing list. My suggestion is to have a monthly drawing for a free gift certificate and the way people get into the drawing is by subscribing to your blog. Once people are subscribed, they will receive email notifications every time you post something new. This is the beginning of establishing yourself as that "expert" we

talked about earlier. Sales are a result of exposure. The more often someone is exposed to your company, the higher probability of them buying from you or referring someone to you.

5. Put a link on your eCommerce site to your blog with a high profile heading that reads "Visit Our Blog for a Chance to Win a $25 Gift Certificate". People love free stuff and they will click that link. Don't forget to put a link to your online store on the blog.

6. Post new content 2-3 times per week (after week one). Doesn't need to be earth-shattering, just interesting, funny, or helpful.

7. Eventually, add a few fun pictures of your dog or have customers email pictures to you. Trust me, put their dog's photo on your blog and they will show up to see it.

That's it! If you can do these few easy steps consistently, you will get repeat visitors and repeat visitors translate into more sales. Never forget that it is easier to get additional business from someone who is already a customer than it is to find a new customer!

If after all of this you are still reluctant or nervous about setting up a blog, or if you just do not have the time, consider having someone get it up and running for you. It will usually run you about $400-500 for this, but that is far better than not having one. Once started, it is extremely easy for you to post and add content.

Remember what I told you about domain names and choosing one that might match search terms within your niche market? It may be too late to change the name of your eCommerce website but now is the perfect time to start a blog and buy a domain name that might help you win high rankings. If your blog ends up outranking your online boutique, great! You'll have links from the blog to the boutique so how you get to page one isn't as important as just getting there. Use Google's Keyword Tool to help you select a domain name for a blog. Look for relevant words that have low competition with 1,000 or more monthly searches.

· · ·

Video Marketing

In the "Getting Started" section, I discussed the value of utilizing videos for product descriptions and demonstrations on your site. Although tremendous benefits exist by making use of videos in this manner, the advantages do not stop there. In fact, when it comes to internet marketing, videos are probably the most under-used and underrated form of media. If you want to be different, if you want to stand out, and if you want to make a big impact, then start using video.

Using Video to Build Rapport

Throughout history, there is one basic business truism that has never faltered or changed. I've already mentioned it, but it's worth more discussion.

People will do business with people that they like and trust!

Take a look at your own spending habits. Do you ever splurge a little bit just because you happen to like the service at one store even though you could get a better price somewhere else? Have you ever gone back to a restaurant where the food is only average, but you enjoy and appreciate the people who work there, the management, or the owners? Have you ever gone out of your way, perhaps driven farther or incurred a minor inconvenience, just to patronize a specific business? You probably buy insurance, home mortgages, real estate, cars, and other higher ticket items from people you know and trust, or at least on the recommendation of someone you know and trust. This trust/credibility relationship is the foundation of nearly every significant business transaction. If you want to build an empire online, you will need to work towards this same high level of trust.

But how to you build confidence and trust online?

Great question! If you think about it, everything I have covered in this book is intended to do exactly that- build the relationship. Articles do it by establishing you as an expert on a topic, blogs do it by providing ongoing contact with your customer base, and now videos add to the equation an element of personality that cannot be expressed through written word. We live in a highly visual society, and we are becoming more and more visual as time passes. Want a few examples of this? Consider how many movies are now made in 3D to enhance the *visual* experience. Think about the impact that websites such as YouTube have made on our culture and how millionaires have been borne out of 60 second videos posted online (Hello Justin Bieber). It's not good enough now for cell phones to simply have a camera, they must have video cameras that shoot in high definition and can stream live to the internet. Some even have two cameras, one for taking pictures/videos and another capable of video chat.

The world is screaming for video at every turn and if you are not providing it, you will likely lose business to those who do. The element of video on your website and blog allows potential customers to relate to you, captures their attention, and keeps them at your site longer (a feat not to be dismissed lightly in a society riddled with Attention Deficit Disorder and an inability to focus and concentrate).

A brief introduction video on your blog with you and your mutt will earn you more trust and credibility with your customers than anything you could possibly write. It allows people to see, hear, and relate to you in a way that only video can. Your online store should also have at least one video, and I recommend putting it on your "About Us" page. There is no better spot for this personal touch.

I began incorporating video into my marketing plan about a year before I started work on this book. Prior to that, I had never owned or used a video camera, nor had I ever uploaded anything to YouTube. Being a complete rookie, I was able to teach myself how to create effective video with just a few simple steps over the course of 7-10 days. If you are not sure how to accomplish this, then follow this process.

1. Go to Target, Wal-Mart, Costco, or any other department store and take a look at the "Flip" brand handheld video cam. It takes great high definition video and costs under $150, but most importantly, it is **very** easy to use- perfect for anyone that is nervous about technology. There are others, but this one has worked perfectly for me. Add a tripod to this for another $15. You don't need anything else.

2. Read through the manual for the camera, this shouldn't take longer than about 5 minutes as there really isn't much to it.

3. Put the camera on the tripod, push record, step in front of it and start talking about something interesting or fun that

happened recently. When you are done with that, record another video where you just spend a few minutes talking about yourself and your background. You'll probably never use these videos, but it will start to get you feeling comfortable talking in front of the video. Keep this in mind- your video does not need to be perfect. Sometimes, "less than perfect" is actually better as people get to see the real you. This human touch will often work wonders.

4. Set up an account with YouTube. Go to www.YouTube.com and follow the directions.

5. The "Flip" camera plugs directly into the USB port of your PC. When you plug it in, it will automatically launch the software with nothing for you to install. Once running, you'll see links at the bottom of the menu for editing, saving to your computer, uploading to YouTube, etc...

Before you know it, you'll be a video veteran.

Using Video to Drive Traffic

Here's something you may not know... Google owns YouTube. They bought it back in 2006 for a reported $1.65 Billion. Yes, that's *billion* with a "*b*". I guess Google thinks that video is important too.

So what?

Well, this simple little fact has some critical implications for your business and marketing strategy. Not only is YouTube owned by Google, but YouTube has also become highly significant and widely used as a search engine. People will actually visit YouTube and search for videos on specific topics.

How can this impact you?

You can use videos as a marketing tool, and since Google views YouTube as a highly relevant and reliable source, posting videos using the proper keywords can lead to high Google rankings. Often, a good video will outrank an article written on the exact same topic.

Here's how it works.

When you upload a video to YouTube, you are allowed to type in a description and keywords for the video. Choose your keywords by utilizing the Keyword Tool that we discussed earlier in the book. Create a description that begins with your full URL (that means include the http:// in front of your web address). Doing this allows people viewing your video to click on the link and go directly to your site and it gives your site an additional backlink which never hurts. This is a great option for someone who feels more comfortable recording a video rather than writing an article. The strategy here is to create video content much like you would an article, perhaps a topic such as tips for potty training your puppy. Make yourself some notes, record the video, post on YouTube, post to your blog, and you will create traffic to your site. Repeat this a couple of times per week with different subject matter and a year from now you won't even recognize your business!

• • •

Pay-Per-Click Advertising

For anyone who is unfamiliar with this method of marketing, I will explain it. Pay-Per-Click (PPC) advertising is the strategy of placing brief yet highly targeted ads on high traffic webpages. Most commonly, you will find PPC on the right hand side of the page when you perform a Google search. They will usually be grouped together under the heading "sponsored links" which simply means that they are not organic listings but rather paid advertisements. The headline of the PPC ad is a clickable link that relocates the browser to your site. When placing a PPC ad, you specify the *exact* keywords where the ad will appear. So, if you want placement under "dog collars", the ad will not appear for the search term "dog**s** collars" as the keywords must be typed exactly in the way you specify.

Once active, you will pay a fee every time someone clicks on your ad, *regardless of how long they remain at your site.* You must be very clear on this concept before you decide to utilize PPC because it is very possible for you to receive hundreds of clicks with no sales and you still are charged for those clicks! The cost per click is determined by the amount you bid when setting the parameters for your ad. The higher you bid, the higher your ad will appear for the search, but beware, these fees can accumulate extremely fast. Unless you have a large budget for advertising, Pay-Per-Click is not something that I would advocate to the neophyte boutique owner. However, should you decide to venture into this realm, investigate all of your options. PPC is available with all the major search engines in addition to outlets such as Facebook, nearly every free email provider (Yahoo, Hotmail, Gmail, etc...), and many other high-traffic sites.

Another form of paid linkage is a flat rate placement for your ad. In this scenario, you would be charged a pre-determined fee each month in exchange for your information appearing on page one for a given search term. The fee varies depending on the popularity of the search (more monthly searches = higher monthly cost). Here's a word of caution with this method. If an advertising agency tells you that the rate per month for placement under "dog clothing" is $500, how will you ever determine if this is a fair price to pay? If you are new to this industry, then you probably will have no clue as to whether you are getting a deal or getting screwed (pardon my French). To help you in this determination, use the following formula:

Monthly Cost of the Ad / Average Profit Per Sale = Number of Sales Needed to Break Even

Applying some real numbers here, if your average profit per sale is $20 and the cost of the ad is $400 per month, then $400/20 = 20$. That means just to break even, your ad must generate 20 sales **that would not have come to you otherwise.** This is a critical concept for you to grasp. If that ad is not generating more than 20 sales from new customers who would have never found your site any other way, then the ad does not make sense and will waste your money.

If you have not been in business long, it may be difficult to figure your average profit per sale. In this case, estimate the average price of a single product on your site, multiply by 40%, and use that number.

Again, I do not recommend this marketing method for the novice website owner unless you have significant experience in the industry coupled with a sizeable budget.

• • •

Attraction/Content Marketing

The concept of Attraction Marketing (sometimes called Content Marketing) interjects a relatively advanced idea into what I intended to be a simple publication. However, it is so vital to online survival that I would be amiss if I failed to discuss it.

The old school method of marketing/advertising can be exemplified by the "barker" (no pun intended) standing outside of the general store in a wild west town. He's proclaiming his magnificent wares to anyone within earshot in hopes that a healthy number of passersby will be willing to part with a few hard-earned dollars based solely on his claims and convincing rhetoric. When we place an advertisement online, in a magazine, or anywhere else, we are essentially doing the same thing. We are trying to capture attention but providing relatively little, if any, value in the process.

Those well versed in Attraction Marketing pursue an entirely different approach by targeting a specific audience, offering needed value, building rapport, and thus earning business by *attracting* people. The difference is similar to hunting vs. fishing. The hunter travels high and low seeking out his prey while the adept fisherman wisely chooses his bait and patiently waits for the prize to come to him. The fisherman actually possesses something that the fish wants... the worm! Over time, business owners that fish develop a following and a database of loyal customers who keep coming back for the worm while the hunter must keep hunting or he will starve.

Attraction Marketing is the present and the future of online marketing as the general public has become immune to the hunters. Think about it, we record our favorite shows so we can fast-forward through commercials, we rarely ever notice the endless number of banner ads on nearly every website, and we delete most emails without reading them. In short, we are tired of being sold so consider this approach- you assemble a well-written article about a topic such as dog clothing using low competition keywords and then publish the article or perhaps even print it on a flyer to pass out in your neighborhood or wherever (get creative). Someone finds your article who happens to be interested in the subject material and they read it. They become impressed with you and your expertise and suddenly find themselves at your website purchasing dog accessories and wanting more information. Continue to do this consistently and you will find yourself with a strong database of loyal customers. The key to successful attraction marketing lies within your ability to provide and disperse **valuable** information. If the content you are creating has little or no value to the reader, you are not only wasting your time, but probably losing customers rather than gaining them. The questions you have to ask yourself when developing an effective attraction marketing campaign are these:

- *"Who are my potential customers?"*

- *"Where are my potential customers?"*

- *"What information would they find to be interesting, valuable, and useful?"*

- *"What is the best way for me to get this information to them?"*

- *"How can I link this information back to me and my website?"*

Does this take time and effort? *Of course it does!* Please do not forget that you are the CEO and if you aren't willing to invest time and effort, no one else will either. This is the difference between a profitable online store (in any niche) and one that fails or barely survives. If you want to build it big, then you will eventually need to adopt the practice of attraction marketing. The good news is that you can utilize attraction marketing in a multitude of ways.

You do not need to have perfect writing skills or be a computer expert. You only need to have your own "worm" and get as many hooks in the water as possible. If you find yourself lacking the time, knowledge, or desire to market in this way, I highly suggest that you outsource this task to a freelance copywriter with some experience in the industry.

• • •

Newsletters

Sit up straight and pay attention because what I'm about to tell you is alone worth the price of this book. *This strategy can earn you hundreds of customers and only about 1% of those that read this will actually do it...* Hopefully you will be in that one percent.

My favorite way of utilizing attraction marketing "off" line is with a newsletter. I find that people love to read short, interesting, fun blubs and articles about pets. The topic can range from pet safety to dog clothing because the truth is that if you have well-placed photos of puppies on the front page of the newsletter, people will pick it up and read it. Of course, you'll get more response from a well written and attractive newsletter than you will from a piece of literature filled with grammatical and spelling errors so it pays to be diligent and get the job done right. Here are a few reasons why I love newsletters...

They give your business credibility

Something about print media seems to carry clout and distinction in our society. Tell someone you have a website these days and they may or may not be impressed, but tell them you publish an educational newsletter and eyebrows will rise. Suddenly they take you a bit more seriously. If your newsletter is a periodical, perhaps monthly, then readers will appreciate and value you and be far more likely to actually visit your website. Traditional advertising in newspapers and magazines is nearly dead unless you have a huge budget for a continuously ongoing marketing campaign. However, having a consistent newsletter will attract loyal followers and increase sales at just a fraction of the cost.

They can be done on a small budget

Most people do not feel very comfortable with their writing skills and cannot see themselves writing a newsletter. If you are in that category, the task can quickly be outsourced for about $300-350. That should acquire a two-page newsletter- front and back of one piece of paper, which is all you need. Getting 1500 color copies can be done using any of the various online printing companies for another $350. That means total production costs out the door are $650-700. How do you pay for it if you don't have $700? Here's the secret... Approach other businesses in your home town that are in the pet industry (and even some that are in different industries.) Tell them that you are publishing a professional newsletter about pet care that will be distributed in the local area and ask if they would like to participate. You will be surprised at the number of positive responses you will get. Dog walkers, dog sitters, groomers, and small pet supply stores that don't directly compete with you are all perfect candidates, but do not forget about other pets such as birds or fish. Find three partners and you are all in for under $200 each! The best part is now you have three additional businesses handing out YOUR information to their customers. Throw in a freebie plug for your local animal shelter and they will be more than willing to display the newsletters too. I have done this a number of times and it always turns into great exposure with very little expense. A small ad for a weekend in a local newspaper could easily cost you more than the newsletter and have nowhere near the same impact.

People keep newsletters longer than flyers

Hand someone a flyer or a business card and you are lucky if it doesn't hit the trash within five minutes. Provide them with a stimulating newsletter and they are likely to take it home, put it on their kitchen counter and not only read it, but perhaps even show it to someone. Your information now has a much greater chance of being seen and utilized. That's powerful stuff!

Articles can be advertisements

Some of the most effective advertisements you will ever see are articles that promote a product or a service. Articles by nature are more informative and carefully worded text will convert far more often than a simple display ad. People are becoming immune to advertising but when it is skillfully crafted as intriguing information readers won't even know they are being "pitched". A perfect example that I love to use is an article on pet safety in automobiles. This wonderful 100 word newsletter article with accompanying picture sells more car safety belts than my employees!

A great way to drive traffic to your website from a newsletter is to promote a drawing for a free gift certificate or something similar. People love to win contests, people love FREE, and there are tons of gamblers out there so this type of promotion appeals to almost everyone. In the next chapter I'll tell you how to set this up on your site but for now, let's just worry about getting people there.

I'll conclude this topic with one final thought. Who reads newsletters about dogs? Dog owners do! Who shops at online dog boutiques? Dog owners do! Talk about hitting your target audience! Print 1500 doggie focused newsletters with your company information and get them out into your community and you are virtually guaranteed that 1500 dog owners will have your web address in their hands. You can't do much better than that.

Since you can hire my company to create the newsletter for you and I've just told you how to make it affordable and why it is so beneficial, there are no excuses left for you to use. Make it a goal to get your first newsletter out within the next 30 days.

• • •

Building a Database

This topic is critical for your long term success with any business. Statistics show that on average, a person will say no to your product or service up to 7 times before they say yes. With that in mind, what are your odds of converting a shopper into a buyer the very first time they visit your site? Not good. That is why you have to do more than just drive traffic to your site. You actually have to figure out a way to get the non-buyers to provide their contact information so you can market to them on a consistent basis. Keeping your name and web address in front of them consistently leads to a higher conversion rate. Sometimes, people just need to know that you are real before they will buy. Direct marketing to this group is a perfect strategy.

But how do you get their information?

Remember a few pages back when I mentioned that contest/giveaway idea? Now is when it has a profound effect on your future. People will not arbitrarily give you their contact information, but they will register online for a contest or a newsletter. Once they voluntarily register, you have the right to send them information unless they specifically tell you not to.

The details...

There are a number of good companies out there that specialize in this form of marketing. The one we use is called GetResponse but there are others. Once you set up an account with them, you can access an online tool to easily build an opt-in form which is then placed on your home page. The form has a spot for name, email address, and any other info you might want (but I always limit it to just name and email). You insert a caption saying something such as *"Register Today for a Chance to Win a $25 Gift Certificate!"* When a customer registers, their information automatically gets stored into a database that you can access at any time. With a couple of easy mouse clicks, you can send out a personalized email to hundreds of people in seconds. Each email has a way for the receiver to "unsubscribe" and that's what makes it legal. However, in my experience, if you keep your emails short and unobtrusive people will rarely unsubscribe. You'll pay roughly $15 per month for this service (cost at the time of this publication) but it is well worth it. Not having a solid strategy for obtaining and maintaining a database is certain death online. It is far too easy for people to visit your site, surf on to the next topic, and then never remember how to get back to you. You don't want to forever be known as "that really great dog clothing site- I just wish I could remember the name!"

The Simple Strategy:

1. Get an account with a company that provides an email marketing/database service and allows you to build a

customized opt-in form. Create a form and put it on your home page.

2. Offer an incentive for people to register (free drawing, newsletter, monthly specials, etc...)

3. Maintain a database of those who register.

4. Send out a minimum of one email every other week to this list. This email should be short and should promote a product or service or provide useful information. Put a direct link to your website in the body of the email. Consider doing this once a week but if you are still working the J.O.B. and time is an issue, then at least every other week will keep your name in front of your audience.

Personally, I find that every time I send out an email to our database, it is good for at least 2-3 retail orders within the first hour after I send it. Is it worth the effort? You bet!

Another great way to add to your database is with your blog. Provide useful and stimulating information and people will not only want to read it, but they will also subscribe to your blog to make sure that they are notified every time you publish a new post. Subscribers to our Doggie Designer blog have increased steadily from day one. At the time of this publication they number around 300 and many look forward with anticipation to our posts. In fact, if we let more than a week go by without adding new content (which seldom happens), emails will pour in asking us when our next post is coming.

Your list is the life-blood of your business. Remember, database building does not happen overnight. It will start slow but with a consistent effort, the list takes shape and begins to snowball. Your efforts will be rewarded and persistency is definitely the key.

• • •

More Marketing Tips on a Budget

You may have already realized that with the exception of pay-per-click (which I did not recommend for new website owners) all of the marketing methods I have discussed in this book are low cost. Many are free such as online article/video marketing and blogs and while there is some expense to developing a newsletter, I have given you a solid strategy for defraying most of it. But just in case that marketing "fire" has yet to ignite within you, I want to throw a few more ideas at you.

• • •

Business Cards

This one is really a no brainer. You own a company, you need to promote yourself, you better have a professional looking business card with your contact information and web address. When you serendipitously meet a dog owner at your local dog park (which undoubtedly will happen), not having a card to hand that person at the end of the conversation is nothing short of negligence on your part. Quickly scribbling the web address on the back of grocery store receipt and offering it to this potential customer screams "rookie" and "amateur". Good luck getting that person to pull out their credit card at your site! There are dozens of online printers where you can get 250 quality business cards for under $20. If you have not done this yet, do it TODAY!

• • •

Postcards

I really like postcards and have had a great deal of success with them in a number of different ways. Postcards not only act as fancy business cards, but can also contain coupons, special offers, custom pictures, product blurbs, and a host of other useful information. One great way to boost repeat sales is to have a postcard printed up that offers a discount or free shipping on the next purchase. Send it out the day you get the customer's initial order. A direct mail postcard can be mailed to a customer 4 times a year for about $1.00. Since they have already done business with you, that's about eight cents per month to keep in touch and solicit additional orders. Just one order earns your investment back 10-20 times or more. Want to boost sales with a new product line you just introduced? Upload a few high resolution images on to a postcard and send it out to your past customers along with a coupon offer. It will result in orders.

Get creative with ways to distribute your postcards. Try approaching a store owner in your town and offer to partner up on printing costs and get postcards made with your business on one side and their business on the other. Most owners would love to cut their advertising expenses and would appreciate the offer, especially if you are offering to hand them out to people. As many of you know, we also own a retail dog boutique in Laguna Beach, California and I spend a great deal of time there. Nothing aggravates me more than when someone walks into my store (where I pay the rent, where I pay the insurance, where I pay the taxes, and where I pay for all of the inventory and upkeep) and asks me if they can display their business cards on my countertop (oh yeah, I pay for that too)! Nine times out of ten this person never even buys products from me, they are just looking for a freebie. PLEASE do not be that person or business owners will resent you as this is a marketing "strategy" used primarily by those who have no idea the proper way to foster a business relationship. However, if any of these people had even an ounce of marketing savvy, they would approach me with an idea that would be mutually beneficial for both me and them! Get it? Co-op advertising benefits you **and** the owner and since I can almost guarantee that no one has ever offered to do this, you may end up making a new friend and some-one who will truly help to promote your site.

Remember this mantra… *Those who succeed in business are those who are successful in helping others to get what they want.* Or, as Zig Ziglar says "Help enough people get what they want and you'll get what you want." If you want a local business to promote your website (and you should) then find a way to help them get what they want too!

Where do you get postcards? I have them made online. Any repu-table online print source such as VistaPrint can provide dozens of different marketing tools and when it comes to postcards, they have templates all ready to go. You just need to type in your text, upload any images, and place the order. Fast, easy, affordable, and professional.

• • •

Use Your Car as a Traveling Billboard

For less than twenty dollars, you can have a custom license plate frame made with your web address on it. Seems like a pretty inexpensive and simple way for you to expose your business to a few people in your local area. If the frame costs you $20 and only 2 people see it every day, that's 730 exposures per year which works out to 2.7 cents per person. You won't find advertising much cheaper than that. For another $30 or so, you can have two vinyl magnetic signs made for your car doors. Do this and now you have increased those exposures to dozens of people every day for under fifty bucks! If you're new and you need web traffic and sales, give this a try. Get lucky and you might just become known around town as the "dog clothes lady/guy"- not a bad nickname for someone trying to build a profitable online dog boutique.

CONCLUSION

The 95/5 Rule

Well, you made it to the end of the book so I guess that means that I haven't scared you too badly. Remember that I told you my goal with this book was to give you the nuts and bolts of what it will take for you to be successful running an online boutique. Yes, there is still a monumental amount of information out there that you could learn and dozens of topics which I purposely omitted from this guide. That's right, *purposely* omitted. Understand that I have been in your shoes (hey, I'm even still wearing them). I am not an internet guru out to sell a million copies of a book with no concern as to whether or not it aids you or confuses you- in fact, quite the opposite. I want the information here to give you an edge on your competition and point you down a path that leads to your goals and dreams and the only way to accomplish that is to keep it simple, concise, and focused. In the beginning stages of your business, it is far more powerful to develop laser focus on one or two strategies rather than attempting to cast a massive net with a "Jack of all trades, master of none" philosophy. Here's why...

In business, and perhaps life in general, there is a rule which many will refer to as the "95/5 Rule". It has endless applications. I remember one of my high school football coaches, who was also an avid fisherman, used to say "5% of the fishermen catch 95% of the fish." In the business world, one might say "5% of the salespeople make 95% of the sales." But there is also another meaning, and this one will determine whether or not you win or lose with your online boutique. The sad truth is that only about 5% of the people who read this book will consistently take the required action and implement these suggested strategies into their business. The other 95% will become increasingly more frustrated with the lack of results until they finally throw in the towel. Granted, many of the 95% will try one or two methods for a short period of time, but then excuses will start kicking in such as "not enough time," "don't understand it," "too difficult," and a host of other back door exit strategies as immediate gratification doesn't materialize. If you give yourself an out, more often than not you'll find yourself taking it, so don't make failure an option. Here's another quote from that same high school football coach, "The only place where *success* comes before *work* is in the dictionary!"

As I have told you already, you are the CEO of your business and victory or failure is completely up to you. The internet is a level playing field where anyone can thrive, if you are willing to pay the price. Unfortunately, too many of us do not realize the price until we are already in the game.

But here's the good news:

ANYONE can be in the 5%! It is 100% up to you. If you are looking for the magic bullet or the secret sauce that will propel your website into heavenly profits overnight, I'm sorry to be the one to pull you back down to reality. That type of rocket ship ride occasionally happens, but for the most part, the success you see others achieve is a result of committed and sustained effort. Now that you know that 95% of people will not make this type of commitment, you should be motivated to do so. Perhaps this little bit of knowledge really is the magic bullet! The biggest difference between the 5% and the 95%? It's not your pricing, it's not your inventory, it's not the aesthetics of your website… it'sYOU. Right now you need to take another look in the mirror and evaluate your level of commitment to this project. Are you willing to do things that the other 95% will not do? Are you willing to learn strategies that the other 95% will never learn? Are you willing to commit the time and effort that the other 95% will not? If you can answer "Yes" to these three questions, then you are in the right place and heading in the right direction, so I congratulate you!

So now what?

I encourage you to go back through the chapters of this book. If you are brand new, then pay careful attention to the "Getting Started" section and make sure that your website is built correctly and your foundation is solid. I will once again stress the importance of having your site created by people who know this industry well, whether it is my company or someone else, experience in this field is so valuable. Making sure that small design details are done properly now can make an enormous impact on your marketing efforts later.

If your site is already up and running, then you need to focus your attention on marketing efforts. Review your site's page descriptions, keywords, categories, and permalinks to assure that you are optimized as well as possible. Then, reread my marketing section to determine the one or two strategies best suited to your time, budget, and talents. Once this is done, get to work. Marketing your site is challenging yet rewarding, and when you start to see your traffic increase, you can be proud of your accomplishment- you'll be in the top 5%.

What to Expect

As you might imagine, the first 12 months is by far the most dif- ficult. The learning curve can be very frustrating if this is your initial online venture. Look at it as if you were back in school. You need to absorb as much as you can, put a plan into action, make a few mistakes, and do your best not to make them more than once. This first year is when the vast majority of the 95% will disappear as the cream rises to the top. You will be tested often, and these tests will come in a variety of forms. I found that reading books on business, marketing, and positive mental attitude helped me to survive year one.

The second 12 months is usually when you will start to experi- ence some growth. If you have done things right so far, you'll be attracting people to your site, accumulating sales, and building a database. This is when that opt-in form on your home page will start to pay off because now you have a list to whom you can send product updates, newsletters, sale promotions, and other adver- tisements reminding them of your presence and encouraging them to shop with you. Your site should be ranking on page one or two for the keywords you are targeting and at the very least, you should be breaking even financially and perhaps even turning a small profit. At this point, you might consider expanding your product line and adding some affiliate links to take advantage of your web traffic. An example of an affiliate link would be establishing a partnership with a large company such as Amazon.com. By setting up an affiliate account with them, you will be able to earn commissions if people go to your site, click on the Amazon link, and make purchases. This allows you to market books, CD's, DVD's and more material within the canine niche and gives you an additional stream of income. Believe me, when you make it to this stage, you are definitely in the 5% group.

Hitting year three and beyond is a wonderful accomplishment as most small businesses from any industry never make it this far. So, get yourself a nice bottle of champagne (or your favorite beverage) and toast to your success- and then get back to work! This is not the time to get lazy, but rather the time to look back, see what enabled you to get this far, and do even more of it. You are excitingly close to that lifestyle you desire so do not get complacent. The gold ring is in sight, so keep working, look for further opportunities to expand and improve, and don't forget the fundamentals. You may be forced soon to evaluate the possibility of quitting the day job as your online business has begun to require more of your attention. At some point, every 5%'er has to make this decision. It's not always easy to give up that steady paycheck, benefits, vacation pay, etc... but this is your dream now becoming a reality. Embrace the unknown and create your own destiny. The sacrifice is great, but the reward is immeasurable. The key is to never lose sight of your goal.

"There are 86,400 seconds in a day. It's up to you to decide what to do with them."

"Failure and rejection are only the first step to succeeding."

"Don't give up, don't ever give up."

Jim Valvano

Hall of Fame College Basketball Coach

North Carolina State University

Online Resources

Building Your Website

www.dog-boutique.net

Hosting Companies for eCommerce

www.volusion.com
www.fortune3.com

Domain Names and/or Hosting for Blogs

www.1and1.com
www.godaddy.com
www.hostgator.com

Email and Database Management/Marketing

www.getresponse.com
www.aweber.com

Blogs

www.wordpress.com
www.wordpress.org

Social Bookmarking Sites

www.digg.com
www.delicious.com
www.stumbleupon.com
www.socialadr.com

Free Article Directories

www.ezinearticles.com
www.articlesbase.com
www.goarticles.com

Video Directories

www.YouTube.com
www.metacafe.com
www.video.google.com
www.dailymotion.com

www.ingramcontent.com/pod-product-compliance
Lightning Source LLC
Chambersburg PA
CBHW051211050326
40689CB00008B/1272